KRAFT
PHILADELPHIA®

A Taste of
Heaven

pil
Publications
International, Ltd.

© 2007 Publications International, Ltd.
Recipes and text © 2007 Kraft Food Holdings

Photography on pages 27, 29, 31, 33, 35, 51, 53, 55, 57, 59, 61, and 95 © 2007 Kraft Food Holdings. All other photography © 2007 Publications International, Ltd.

ISBN-13: 978-1-4127-2836-2
ISBN-10: 1-4127-2836-3

Manufactured in China.

Pictured on the front cover: New York Cheesecake *(page 39)*.

Pictured on the back cover *(clockwise from top)*: Chocolate Cheesecakes for Two *(page 34)*, "Fruit Smoothie" No-Bake Cheesecake *(page 12)*, Baked Crab Rangoon *(page 88)* .

Microwave Cooking: Microwave ovens vary in wattage. Use the cooking times as guidelines and check for doneness before adding more time.

Preparation/Cooking Times: Preparation times are based on the approximate amount of time required to assemble the recipe before cooking, baking, chilling, or serving. These times include preparation steps such as measuring, chopping, and mixing. The fact that some preparations and cooking can be done simultaneously is taken into account. Preparation of optional ingredients and serving suggestions is not included.

CONTENTS

62

34

40

65

A TASTE OF HEAVEN

PHILADELPHIA CREAM CHEESE
TIPS FOR THE PERFECT CHEESECAKE

For best quality and results, always use **PHILADELPHIA** Cream Cheese.

Preheating the oven: The baking time indicated in a recipe is based on using a preheated oven. Turn the oven on when you start to mix the cheesecake ingredients. This should allow enough time for the oven to heat to the correct temperature for when you are ready to place the cheesecake in the oven to bake. Unless otherwise indicated, always bake cheesecakes in the center of the middle oven rack.

Beating the batter: While adding ingredients, do not overbeat the cheesecake batter. Too much air beaten into the batter will result in a cheesecake that sinks in the center when cooled.

Baking cheesecakes: Overbaked cheesecakes tend to crack. Remove the cheesecake from the oven when the center is almost set (i.e. center of cheesecake still wiggles when the pan is gently shaken from side-to-side). Although the cheesecake appears underbaked, the residual heat in the cheesecake will be enough to finish baking the center. After chilling, the cheesecake will have a perfectly smooth consistency.

Cooling cheesecakes: Cool cheesecakes completely before refrigerating. Placing a warm cheesecake in the refrigerator will cause condensation to form on the cake, resulting in a soggy cheesecake.

Cutting cheesecakes: Cut cheesecakes when they are cold rather than warm. Use a sharp knife with a clean, thin blade. To make clean cuts, dip the knife in hot water after each cut and wipe the blade clean.

For all of your occasions, *PHILLY* MAKES A BETTER CHEESECAKE.

*During tests of plain New York-style cheesecake made with **PHILADELPHIA** Cream Cheese versus store-brand versions, consumers rated PHILLY cheesecake as better tasting.*

HOW TO BAKE IN A SPRINGFORM PAN: *Preheat oven to 325°F if using a silver 9-inch springform pan (or to 300° F if using a dark nonstick 9-inch springform pan). Prepare crust as directed; press firmly onto bottom of pan. Prepare filling as directed; pour over crust. Bake 1 hour or until center is almost set. Run small knife or small spatula around rim of pan to loosen cake; cool before removing rim of pan. Refrigerate 4 hours or overnight.*

New York-Style Sour Cream-Topped Cheesecake *(page 62)*

FRESH FRUIT CHEESECAKES

CHEESECAKES PAIRED WITH THE FRESH FRUITS AND FLAVORS OF SUMMER

Lemon Cheesecake

Prep: 15 minutes plus refrigerating • Bake: 50 minutes

1½ cups **HONEY MAID** Graham Cracker Crumbs

⅓ cup sugar

⅓ cup butter or margarine, melted

3 packages (8 ounces each) **PHILADELPHIA** Cream Cheese, softened

1 cup sugar

1 cup **BREAKSTONE'S** or **KNUDSEN** Sour Cream

3 eggs

Grated peel and juice from 1 lemon

PREHEAT oven to 325°F if using a silver 9-inch springform pan (or to 300°F if using a dark nonstick 9-inch springform pan). Mix graham crumbs, ⅓ cup sugar and butter. Reserve ½ cup crumb mixture; press remaining crumb mixture firmly onto bottom of pan. Set aside.

BEAT cream cheese and 1 cup sugar in large bowl with electric mixer on medium speed until well blended. Add sour cream; mix well. Add eggs, 1 at a time, mixing on low speed after each addition just until blended. Stir in lemon peel and juice. Pour over crust; sprinkle with reserved crumb mixture.

BAKE 45 to 50 minutes or until center is almost set. Run knife or metal spatula around rim of pan to loosen cake; cool before removing rim. Refrigerate at least 4 hours or overnight. Store leftover cheesecake in refrigerator.

Makes 12 servings.

HOW TO SOFTEN CREAM CHEESE:

Place unwrapped package of cream cheese in microwaveable bowl. Microwave on HIGH (100%) 15 seconds or just until softened. Add 15 seconds for each additional package of cream cheese.

SIZE-WISE:

Looking for a special dessert? Enjoy 1 serving of this elegant lemon cheesecake.

Triple Citrus Cheesecake

Prep: 30 minutes plus refrigerating • Bake: 1 hour 5 minutes

 1 cup **HONEY MAID** Graham Cracker Crumbs

⅓ cup firmly packed brown sugar

¼ cup (½ stick) butter or margarine, melted

 4 packages (8 ounces each) **PHILADELPHIA** Cream Cheese, softened

 1 cup granulated sugar

 2 tablespoons flour

 1 teaspoon vanilla

 4 eggs

 1 tablespoon fresh lemon juice

 1 tablespoon fresh lime juice

 1 tablespoon fresh orange juice

 1 teaspoon grated lemon peel

 1 teaspoon grated lime peel

 1 teaspoon grated orange peel

PREHEAT oven to 325°F if using a silver 9-inch springform pan (or to 300°F if using a dark nonstick 9-inch springform pan). Mix crumbs, brown sugar and butter; press firmly onto bottom of pan. Bake 10 minutes.

BEAT cream cheese, granulated sugar, flour and vanilla with electric mixer on medium speed until well blended. Add eggs, 1 at a time, mixing on low speed after each addition just until blended. Stir in remaining ingredients; pour over crust.

BAKE 1 hour and 5 minutes or until center is almost set. Run knife or metal spatula around rim of pan to loosen cake; cool before removing rim of pan. Refrigerate 4 hours or overnight. Store leftover cheesecake in refrigerator.

Makes 16 servings.

Fruit Pizza

Prep: 25 minutes plus refrigerating

- **1** package (20 ounces) refrigerated sliceable sugar cookies, sliced
- **1** package (8 ounces) **PHILADELPHIA** Cream Cheese, softened
- **¼** cup sugar
- **½** teaspoon vanilla
-   Assorted fruit, such as sliced kiwi, strawberries, blueberries and drained, canned mandarin orange segments
- **¼** cup apricot preserves, pressed through sieve to remove lumps
- **1** tablespoon water

PREHEAT oven to 375°F. Line 12-inch pizza pan with foil; spray with cooking spray. Arrange cookie dough slices in single layer in prepared pan; press together to form crust. Bake 14 minutes; cool. Invert onto serving plate; carefully remove foil. Invert onto large serving plate or tray so crust is right-side-up.

BEAT cream cheese, sugar and vanilla with electric mixer on medium speed until well blended. Spread over crust.

ARRANGE fruit over cream cheese layer. Mix preserves and water; brush over fruit. Refrigerate 2 hours. Cut into 12 wedges to serve. Store leftover dessert in refrigerator.

Makes 12 servings, 1 wedge each.

"Fruit Smoothie" No-Bake Cheesecake

Prep: 15 minutes plus refrigerating

1½ cups **HONEY MAID** Graham Cracker Crumbs

¼ cup (½ stick) butter, melted

2 tablespoons sugar

4 packages (8 ounces each) **PHILADELPHIA** Neufchâtel Cheese,
   ⅓ Less Fat than Cream Cheese, softened

½ cup sugar

1 package (12 ounces) frozen mixed berries (strawberries, raspberries,
   blueberries and blackberries), thawed, drained

1 tub (8 ounces) **COOL WHIP LITE** Whipped Topping, thawed, divided

LINE 13×9-inch baking pan with foil, with ends of foil extending over sides of pan. Mix graham crumbs, butter and 2 tablespoons sugar; press firmly onto bottom of prepared pan. Refrigerate while preparing filling.

BEAT Neufchâtel cheese and ½ cup sugar in large bowl with electric mixer on medium speed until well blended. Smash drained berries with fork; stir into cheese mixture. Gently stir in 2 cups of the whipped topping. Spoon over crust; cover.

REFRIGERATE 4 hours or until firm. Use foil handles to remove cheesecake from pan before cutting into pieces to serve. Top with the remaining whipped topping. Store leftover cheesecake in refrigerator.

Makes 16 servings, 1 piece each.

VARIATION:

Omit mixed frozen berries. Add 3 cups fresh mixed berries and additional ¼ cup sugar to Neufchâtel cheese mixture, mixing with electric mixer on medium speed until well blended.

KRAFT PHILADELPHIA

EASY & ELEGANT DESSERTS

SIMPLE, SENSATIONAL TREATS

OREO No-Bake Cheesecake

Prep: 15 minutes plus refrigerating

- **1** package (1 pound 2 ounces) **OREO** Chocolate Sandwich Cookies, divided
- **¼** cup (½ stick) butter, melted
- **4** packages (8 ounces each) **PHILADELPHIA** Cream Cheese, softened
- **½** cup sugar
- **1** teaspoon vanilla
- **1** tub (8 ounces) **COOL WHIP** Whipped Topping, thawed

LINE 13×9-inch pan with foil, with ends of foil extending over sides of pan. Coarsely chop 15 of the cookies; set aside. Finely crush remaining cookies; mix with butter. Press firmly onto bottom of prepared pan. Refrigerate while preparing filling.

BEAT cream cheese, sugar and vanilla in large bowl with electric mixer on medium speed until well blended. Gently stir in whipped topping and chopped cookies. Spoon over crust; cover.

REFRIGERATE 4 hours or until firm. Store leftover cheesecake in refrigerator.

Makes 16 servings, 1 piece each.

VARIATION:

Prepare as directed, using 1 package (1 pound 2 ounces) Golden OREO Chocolate Creme Sandwich Cookies or 1 package (17 ounces) OREO DOUBLE STUF Cool Mint Creme Sandwich Cookies.

Key Lime Cheesecake Pie

Prep: 25 minutes plus refrigerating

1¼ cups finely crushed coconut bar cookies

¼ cup (½ stick) butter or margarine, melted

3 tablespoons sugar

2 packages (8 ounces each) **PHILADELPHIA** Cream Cheese, softened

1 can (14 ounces) sweetened condensed milk

½ teaspoon grated lime peel

⅓ cup lime juice

Few drops green food coloring (optional)

PREHEAT oven to 350°F. Mix crumbs, butter and sugar; press firmly onto bottom and up side of 9-inch pie plate. Bake 10 minutes. Cool.

BEAT cream cheese and sweetened condensed milk in large bowl with electric mixer on medium speed until well blended. Add peel, juice and food coloring; mix well. Pour into crust.

REFRIGERATE at least 8 hours or overnight. Store leftover pie in refrigerator.

Makes 10 servings.

HOW TO SOFTEN CREAM CHEESE:

Place unwrapped package of cream cheese in microwaveable bowl. Microwave on HIGH (100%) 15 seconds or just until softened. Add 15 seconds for each additional package of cream cheese.

easy & elegant desserts

Fluffy Cheesecake

Prep: 15 minutes plus refrigerating

- 1 package (8 ounces) **PHILADELPHIA** Cream Cheese, softened
- ⅓ cup sugar
- 1 tub (8 ounces) **COOL WHIP** Whipped Topping, thawed
- 1 **HONEY MAID** Graham Pie Crust (6 ounces)
- 1 apple, cored, thinly sliced (optional)

BEAT cream cheese and sugar in large bowl with wire whisk or electric mixer until well blended. Gently stir in whipped topping.

SPOON into crust.

REFRIGERATE 3 hours or until set. Top with apple slices just before serving.

Makes 8 servings.

FLUFFY CHEESECAKE SQUARES:

Omit pie crust. Mix 1 cup HONEY MAID Graham Cracker Crumbs, 2 tablespoons sugar and ⅓ cup melted butter or margarine. Press onto bottom of foil-lined 8-inch square baking pan. Continue as directed. Makes 9 servings.

FLUFFY CHERRY CHEESECAKE:

Omit apple. Prepare and refrigerate as directed. Top with 1½ cups cherry pie filling just before serving.

Cream Cheese Frosting

Prep: 10 minutes

- **1** package (8 ounces) **PHILADELPHIA** Cream Cheese, softened
- **¼** cup (½ stick) butter or margarine, softened
- **1** teaspoon vanilla
- **1** package (16 ounces) powdered sugar (about 4 cups), sifted

BEAT cream cheese, butter and vanilla in large bowl with electric mixer on medium speed until well blended.

ADD sugar gradually, beating until well blended after each addition.

Makes about 2½ cups or 20 servings, 2 tablespoons each.

NOTE:

Recipe makes enough to fill and frost 2 (8- or 9-inch) cake layers or top and sides of 13×9-inch cake or tops of 24 cupcakes.

COOKING KNOW-HOW:

Sift the powdered sugar before adding to the cream cheese mixture for a smoother frosting.

easy & elegant desserts

Summer Berry Trifle

Prep: 40 minutes plus refrigerating

- 1 cup boiling water
- 1 package (8-serving size) **JELL-O** Brand Strawberry Flavor Gelatin
  Ice cubes
- ½ cup cold water
- 2 cups mixed berries (raspberries, blueberries, strawberries)
- 1 package (8 ounces) **PHILADELPHIA** Cream Cheese, softened
- 1¼ cups cold milk, divided
- 1 package (4-serving size) **JELL-O** Cheesecake or Vanilla Flavor Instant Pudding & Pie Filling
- 1 tub (8 ounces) **COOL WHIP** Strawberry Whipped Topping, thawed
- 1 package (10.75 ounces) pound cake, cubed

STIR boiling water into dry gelatin in large bowl at least 2 minutes until completely dissolved. Add enough ice to cold water to measure 1 cup. Add to gelatin; stir until ice is completely melted. Let stand about 15 minutes or until thickened. (Spoon drawn through gelatin leaves definite impression.) Stir in berries.

PLACE cream cheese in large bowl; beat with wire whisk until creamy. Gradually add ¼ cup of the milk, beating until well blended. Add remaining 1 cup milk and dry pudding mix; beat 2 minutes or until well blended. Gently stir in whipped topping. Set aside.

PLACE about half of the cake cubes in bottom of large serving bowl; cover with half of the pudding mixture. Top with layers of the gelatin mixture, remaining cake cubes and remaining pudding mixture. Refrigerate at least 1 hour or until ready to serve. Store leftover dessert in refrigerator.

Makes 18 servings.

JAZZ IT UP:

Garnish with additional berries just before serving.

VARIATION:

Prepare as directed, using JELL-O Brand Strawberry Flavor Sugar Free Low Calorie Gelatin, COOL WHIP LITE Whipped Topping and reduced fat or fat free pound cake.

Creamy Lemon Nut Bars

Prep: 20 minutes plus cooling • Bake: 30 minutes

½ cup (1 stick) butter or margarine, softened

⅓ cup powdered sugar

2 teaspoons vanilla

1¾ cups flour, divided

⅓ cup **PLANTERS** Pecans, chopped

1 package (8 ounces) **PHILADELPHIA** Cream Cheese, softened

2 cups granulated sugar

3 eggs

½ cup lemon juice

1 tablespoon grated lemon peel

1 tablespoon powdered sugar

PREHEAT oven to 350°F. Line 13×9-inch baking pan with foil; spray with cooking spray. Mix butter, ⅓ cup powdered sugar and vanilla in large bowl. Gradually stir in 1½ cups of the flour and pecans. Press dough firmly onto bottom of prepared pan. Bake 15 minutes.

BEAT cream cheese and granulated sugar in medium bowl with electric mixer on high speed until well blended. Add remaining ¼ cup flour and eggs; beat until blended.

STIR in lemon juice and peel. Pour over baked crust in pan. Bake 30 minutes or until set. Remove from oven; cool completely. Sprinkle with 1 tablespoon powdered sugar; cut into 32 bars.

Makes 32 servings, 1 bar each.

HOW TO GRATE CITRUS PEEL:

Always wash and dry citrus fruit before grating. Move whole citrus fruit up and down on the side of the grater with the smallest holes to remove ONLY the surface of the fruit peel. (The inner white part is bitter.) Continue to grate fruit until you have the desired amount of grated peel, rotating fruit on the grater as necessary. Use this technique for grating any citrus fruit.

SUBSTITUTE:

Prepare as directed, using lime juice and grated lime peel.

3-STEP Mini Cheesecakes

Prep: 10 minutes plus refrigerating

- 2 packages (8 ounces each) **PHILADELPHIA** Cream Cheese, softened
- ½ cup sugar
- ½ teaspoon vanilla
- 2 eggs
- 12 **OREO** Chocolate Sandwich Cookies
- 1 kiwi, peeled, cut into 6 slices
- 36 blueberries (about ½ cup)
- 12 raspberries (about ⅓ cup)

PREHEAT oven to 350°F. Beat cream cheese, sugar and vanilla in large bowl with electric mixer on medium speed until well blended. Add eggs, 1 at a time, beating on low speed after each addition just until blended.

PLACE 1 cookie in bottom of each of 12 medium paper-lined muffin cups. Fill evenly with batter.

BAKE 20 minutes or until centers are almost set. Cool. Refrigerate 3 hours or overnight. Cut kiwi slices in half. Top each cheesecake with 1 kiwi half, 3 blueberries and 1 raspberry just before serving.

Makes 12 servings.

CHEESECAKE SQUARES:

Line 8-inch square baking pan with foil. Mix 1½ cups finely crushed OREO Chocolate Sandwich Cookies or HONEY MAID Honey Grahams with ¼ cup melted butter; press firmly onto bottom of pan. Prepare cheesecake batter as directed. Pour over crust. Bake and refrigerate as directed. Cut into 16 squares. Top evenly with the fruit mixture just before serving. Makes 16 servings, 1 square each.

Marble Brownies

Prep: 20 minutes • Bake: 40 minutes

- **1** package (20.5 ounces) brownie mix (do not use mixes that include a syrup pouch)
- **1** package (8 ounces) **PHILADELPHIA** Cream Cheese, softened
- ⅓ cup sugar
- **1** egg
- ½ teaspoon vanilla
- ½ cup **BAKER'S** Semi-Sweet Chocolate Chunks

PREHEAT oven to 350°F. Prepare brownie mix as directed on package; spread into greased 13×9-inch baking pan.

BEAT cream cheese with electric mixer on medium speed until smooth. Add sugar, mixing until well blended. Add egg and vanilla; mix just until blended.

POUR cream cheese mixture over brownie batter; cut through batter with knife several times for marble effect. Sprinkle with chocolate chunks.

BAKE 35 to 40 minutes or until cream cheese mixture is lightly browned. Cool; cut into squares.

Makes 32 servings, 1 square each.

SUBSTITUTE:

Prepare as directed, using PHILADELPHIA Neufchâtel Cheese, ⅓ Less Fat than Cream Cheese.

JAZZ IT UP:

After brownies have cooled, use a small, round cookie cutter, about 1 inch in diameter, to cut small, delicate petit four-type brownies.

American Berry No-Bake Cheesecake

Prep: 15 minutes plus refrigerating

- 2 packages (8 ounces each) **PHILADELPHIA** Cream Cheese, softened
- ⅓ cup sugar
- 2 cups thawed **COOL WHIP** Whipped Topping
- 1 **HONEY MAID** Graham Pie Crust (6 ounces)
- 1 pint (2 cups) strawberries, halved
- ⅓ cup blueberries

BEAT cream cheese and sugar in large bowl with electric mixer on medium speed until well blended. Gently stir in whipped topping.

SPOON into crust.

REFRIGERATE 3 hours or until set. Arrange strawberries and blueberries in rows on top of cheesecake to resemble flag. (Or arrange fruit in other desired design on top of cheesecake.) Store leftover cheesecake in refrigerator.

Makes 8 servings.

HEALTHY LIVING:

Looking for a reduced fat version of this summertime favorite? Save 10 grams of total fat, 6 grams of saturated fat and 90 calories per serving by preparing with PHILADELPHIA Neufchâtel Cheese, ⅓ Less Fat than Cream Cheese; COOL WHIP LITE Whipped Topping and a ready-to-use reduced fat graham cracker crumb crust (for a delicious 320 calories and 19 grams of fat per serving).

BEST OF SEASON:

Omit strawberries and blueberries. Prepare cheesecake as directed. Top with 2⅓ cups combined fresh raspberries and sliced peaches.

easy & elegant desserts

3-STEP Luscious Lemon Cheesecake

Prep: 10 minutes plus refrigerating • Bake: 40 minutes

- 2 packages (8 ounces each) **PHILADELPHIA** Cream Cheese, softened
- ½ cup sugar
- ½ teaspoon grated lemon peel
- 1 tablespoon fresh lemon juice
- ½ teaspoon vanilla
- 2 eggs
- 1 **HONEY MAID** Graham Pie Crust (6 ounces)

PREHEAT oven to 350°F. Beat cream cheese, sugar, peel, juice and vanilla with electric mixer on medium speed until well blended. Add eggs; mix just until blended.

POUR into crust.

BAKE 40 minutes or until center is almost set. Cool. Refrigerate at least 3 hours or overnight. Store leftover cheesecake in refrigerator.

Makes 8 servings.

VARIATION:

Prepare as directed, substituting lime juice for the lemon juice and grated lime peel for the lemon peel.

Chocolate Cheesecakes for Two

Prep: 10 minutes plus refrigerating

- 2 ounces (¼ of 8-ounce package) **PHILADELPHIA** Cream Cheese, softened
- 1 tablespoon sugar
- 1 square **BAKER'S** Semi-Sweet Baking Chocolate, melted
- ½ cup thawed **COOL WHIP** Whipped Topping
- 2 **OREO** Chocolate Sandwich Cookies

BEAT cream cheese, sugar and chocolate in medium bowl with wire whisk until well blended. Add whipped topping; mix well.

PLACE 1 cookie on bottom of each of 2 paper-lined medium muffin cups; fill evenly with cream cheese mixture.

REFRIGERATE 2 hours or overnight. (Or, if you are in a hurry, place in the freezer for 1 hour.)

Makes 2 servings.

JAZZ IT UP:

Dust surface with cocoa powder. Top with heart-shaped stencil; dust with powdered sugar.

Banana Split Cake

Prep: 15 minutes plus refrigerating

1½ cups **HONEY MAID** Graham Cracker Crumbs

1 cup sugar, divided

⅓ cup butter, melted

2 packages (8 ounces each) **PHILADELPHIA** Cream Cheese, softened

1 can (20 ounces) crushed pineapple, drained

6 medium bananas, divided

2 cups cold milk

2 packages (4-serving size each) **JELL-O** Vanilla Flavor Instant Pudding & Pie Filling

2 cups thawed **COOL WHIP** Whipped Topping, divided

1 cup **PLANTERS** Chopped Pecans

MIX crumbs, ¼ cup of the sugar and the butter; press firmly onto bottom of 13×9-inch pan. Freeze 10 minutes.

BEAT cream cheese and remaining ¾ cup sugar with electric mixer on medium speed until well blended. Spread carefully over crust; top with pineapple. Slice 4 of the bananas; arrange over pineapple.

POUR milk into medium bowl. Add dry pudding mixes. Beat with wire whisk 2 minutes or until well blended. Gently stir in 1 cup of the whipped topping; spread over banana layer in pan. Top with remaining 1 cup whipped topping; sprinkle with pecans. Refrigerate 5 hours. Slice remaining 2 bananas just before serving; arrange over dessert. Store any leftover dessert in refrigerator.

Makes 24 servings, 1 piece each.

SUBSTITUTE:

Prepare as directed, using PHILADELPHIA Neufchâtel Cheese, ⅓ Less Fat than Cream Cheese; JELL-O Vanilla Flavor Fat Free Sugar Free Instant Reduced Calorie Pudding & Pie Filling; and COOL WHIP LITE Whipped Topping.

KRAFT PHILADELPHIA

BEST-LOVED
CHEESECAKES

TIMELESS, CLASSIC CHEESECAKES
EVERYONE WILL LOVE

New York Cheesecake

Prep: 15 minutes plus refrigerating • Bake: 40 minutes

- 1 cup crushed **HONEY MAID** Honey Grahams (about 6 grahams)
- 3 tablespoons sugar
- 3 tablespoons butter or margarine, melted
- 5 packages (8 ounces each) **PHILADELPHIA** Cream Cheese, softened
- 1 cup sugar
- 3 tablespoons flour
- 1 tablespoon vanilla
- 1 cup **BREAKSTONE'S** or **KNUDSEN** Sour Cream
- 4 eggs
- 1 can (21 ounces) cherry pie filling

PREHEAT oven to 325°F. Mix crumbs, 3 tablespoons sugar and butter; press firmly onto bottom of 13×9-inch baking pan. Bake 10 minutes.

BEAT cream cheese, 1 cup sugar, flour and vanilla with electric mixer on medium speed until well blended. Add sour cream; mix well. Add eggs, 1 at a time, mixing on low speed after each addition just until blended. Pour over crust.

BAKE 40 minutes or until center is almost set. Cool completely. Refrigerate at least 4 hours or overnight. Top with pie filling before serving. Store leftover cheesecake in refrigerator.

Makes 16 servings, 1 slice each.

JAZZ IT UP:

Omit pie filling. Arrange 2 cups mixed berries on top of chilled cheesecake. Brush with 2 tablespoons melted strawberry jelly.

Brownie Cheesecake

Prep: 15 minutes plus refrigerating • Bake: 40 minutes

- 1 package (19 to 21 ounces) brownie mix (13×9-inch pan size)
- 4 packages (8 ounces each) **PHILADELPHIA** Cream Cheese, softened
- 1 cup sugar
- 1 teaspoon vanilla
- ½ cup **BREAKSTONE'S** or **KNUDSEN** Sour Cream
- 3 eggs
- 2 squares **BAKER'S** Semi-Sweet Baking Chocolate

PREHEAT oven to 325°F. Spray 13×9-inch baking pan with cooking spray. Prepare brownie batter as directed on package; pour into prepared pan. Bake 25 minutes or until top of brownie is shiny and center is almost set.

MEANWHILE, beat cream cheese, sugar and vanilla in large bowl with electric mixer on medium speed until well blended. Add sour cream; mix well. Add eggs, 1 at a time, mixing on low speed after each addition just until blended. Gently pour over brownie layer in pan. (Filling will come almost to top of pan.)

BAKE 40 minutes or until center is almost set. Run knife or metal spatula around rim of pan to loosen side of dessert from pan; cool. Refrigerate at least 4 hours or overnight.

MELT chocolate as directed on package; drizzle over cheesecake. Refrigerate 15 minutes or until chocolate is firm. Cut cheesecake into 16 pieces to serve. Store any leftover cheesecake in refrigerator.

Makes 16 servings, 1 piece each.

New York-Style Strawberry Swirl Cheesecake

Prep: 15 minutes plus refrigerating • Bake: 40 minutes

- 1 cup **HONEY MAID** Graham Cracker Crumbs
- 3 tablespoons sugar
- 3 tablespoons butter, melted
- 5 packages (8 ounces each) **PHILADELPHIA** Cream Cheese, softened
- 1 cup sugar
- 3 tablespoons flour
- 1 tablespoon vanilla
- 1 cup **BREAKSTONE'S** or **KNUDSEN** Sour Cream
- 4 eggs
- ⅓ cup **SMUCKER'S**® Seedless Strawberry Jam

PREHEAT oven to 325°F. Line 13×9-inch baking pan with foil, with ends of foil extending over sides of pan. Mix cracker crumbs, 3 tablespoons sugar and butter; press firmly onto bottom of prepared pan. Bake 10 minutes.

BEAT cream cheese, 1 cup sugar, flour and vanilla in large bowl with electric mixer on medium speed until well blended. Add sour cream; mix well. Add eggs, 1 at a time, mixing on low speed after each addition just until blended. Pour over crust. Gently drop small spoonfuls of jam over batter; cut through batter several times with knife for marble effect.

BAKE 40 minutes or until center is almost set. Cool completely. Refrigerate at least 4 hours or overnight. Lift cheesecake from pan using foil handles. Cut into 16 pieces to serve. Store leftover cheesecake in refrigerator.

Makes 16 servings, 1 piece each.

SUBSTITUTE:

Substitute 1 bag (16 ounces) frozen fruit, thawed, drained and puréed, for the ⅓ cup jam.

HEALTHY LIVING:

Save 80 calories, 10 grams of fat and 6 grams of saturated fat per serving by preparing with PHILADELPHIA Neufchâtel Cheese, ⅓ Less Fat than Cream Cheese and BREAKSTONE'S Reduced Fat or KNUDSEN Light Sour Cream (for a delicious 340 calories and 21 grams of fat per serving).

SMUCKER'S is a registered trademark owned and licensed by J.M. Smucker Company.

Blueberry Swirl Cheesecake

Prep: 15 minutes plus refrigerating • Bake: 45 minutes

- 1 cup **HONEY MAID** Graham Cracker Crumbs
- 1 cup plus 3 tablespoons sugar, divided
- 3 tablespoons butter or margarine, melted
- 4 packages (8 ounces each) **PHILADELPHIA** Cream Cheese, softened
- 1 teaspoon vanilla
- 1 cup **BREAKSTONE'S** or **KNUDSEN** Sour Cream
- 4 eggs
- 2 cups fresh or thawed frozen blueberries

PREHEAT oven to 325°F. Mix crumbs, 3 tablespoons of the sugar and butter. Press firmly onto bottom of foil-lined 13×9-inch baking pan. Bake 10 minutes.

BEAT cream cheese, remaining 1 cup sugar and vanilla in large bowl with electric mixer on medium speed until well blended. Add sour cream; mix well. Add eggs, 1 at a time, beating on low speed after each addition just until blended. Pour over crust. Purée blueberries in a blender or food processor. Gently drop spoonfuls of puréed blueberries over batter; cut through batter several times with knife for marble effect.

BAKE 45 minutes or until center is almost set; cool. Cover and refrigerate at least 4 hours before serving. Store leftover cheesecake in refrigerator.

Makes 16 servings.

SUBSTITUTE:

Substitute 1 can (15 ounces) blueberries, well drained, for the 2 cups fresh or frozen blueberries.

MAKE IT EASY:

Instead of using a blender, crush the blueberries in a bowl with a fork. Drain before spooning over the cheesecake batter and swirling to marbleize as directed.

Caramel-Pecan Cheesecake Bars

Prep: 15 minutes plus refrigerating • Bake: 40 minutes

1½ cups **NABISCO** Graham Cracker Crumbs

1 cup coarsely chopped **PLANTERS** Pecans, divided

2 tablespoons granulated sugar

¼ cup (½ stick) butter, melted

4 packages (8 ounces each) **PHILADELPHIA** Cream Cheese, softened

1 cup firmly packed brown sugar

2 tablespoons flour

½ cup **BREAKSTONE'S** or **KNUDSEN** Sour Cream

1 tablespoon vanilla

3 eggs

1 bag (14 ounces) **KRAFT** Caramels, divided

PREHEAT oven to 350°F. Line 13×9-inch baking pan with foil, with ends of foil extending over sides of pan. Mix graham crumbs, ½ cup pecans, granulated sugar and butter; press firmly onto bottom of prepared pan. Bake 10 minutes.

BEAT cream cheese, brown sugar and flour in large bowl with electric mixer on medium speed until well blended. Add sour cream and vanilla; mix well. Add eggs, 1 at a time, mixing on low speed after each addition just until blended. Place 36 of the caramels and 1 tablespoon water in microwaveable bowl. Microwave on HIGH (100%) 1 minute or until caramels are completely melted when stirred. Add to cream cheese batter; stir until well blended. Pour over crust.

BAKE 40 minutes or until center is almost set. Sprinkle cheesecake with remaining ½ cup pecans. Refrigerate at least 4 hours or overnight.

PLACE remaining caramels and additional 1 tablespoon water in microwaveable bowl. Microwave on HIGH (100%) 1 minute or until caramels are completely melted when stirred. Drizzle over cheesecake; let stand until set. Remove dessert from pan using foil handles; cut into 32 bars to serve. Store leftover bars in refrigerator.

Makes 32 servings, 1 bar each.

Chocolate Vanilla Swirl Cheesecake

Prep: 15 minutes plus refrigerating • Bake: 40 minutes

20 **OREO** Chocolate Sandwich Cookies, crushed (about 2 cups)

3 tablespoons butter, melted

4 packages (8 ounces each) **PHILADELPHIA** Cream Cheese, softened

1 cup sugar

1 teaspoon vanilla

1 cup **BREAKSTONE'S** or **KNUDSEN** Sour Cream

4 eggs

6 squares **BAKER'S** Semi-Sweet Baking Chocolate, melted, cooled

PREHEAT oven to 325°F. Line 13×9-inch baking pan with foil, with ends of foil extending over sides of pan. Mix cookie crumbs and butter; press firmly onto bottom of prepared pan. Bake 10 minutes

BEAT cream cheese, sugar and vanilla in large bowl with electric mixer on medium speed until well blended. Add sour cream; mix well. Add eggs, 1 at a time, beating on low speed after each addition just until blended. Remove 1 cup of the batter; set aside. Stir melted chocolate into remaining batter. Pour chocolate batter over crust; top with spoonfuls of remaining plain batter. Cut through batters with knife several times for swirled effect.

BAKE 40 minutes or until center is almost set. Cool. Refrigerate at least 4 hours or overnight. Use foil handles to lift cheesecake from pan before cutting to serve. Store any leftover cheesecake in refrigerator.

Makes 16 servings, 1 piece each.

JAZZ IT UP:

Garnish with chocolate curls just before serving. Use a vegetable peeler to shave the side of an additional square of BAKER'S Semi-Sweet Baking Chocolate and a square of BAKER'S Premium White Baking Chocolate until desired amount of curls are obtained. Wrap remaining chocolate and store at room temperature for another use.

Black Forest Cheesecake

Prep: 15 minutes plus refrigerating • Bake: 40 minutes

20 **OREO** Chocolate Sandwich Cookies, crushed (about 2 cups)

3 tablespoons butter, melted

4 packages (8 ounces each) **PHILADELPHIA** Cream Cheese, softened

1 cup sugar

1 teaspoon vanilla

1 cup **BREAKSTONE'S** or **KNUDSEN** Sour Cream

6 squares **BAKER'S** Semi-Sweet Baking Chocolate, melted

4 eggs

2 cups thawed **COOL WHIP** Whipped Topping

1 can (21 ounces) cherry pie filling

PREHEAT oven to 325°F. Line 13×9-inch baking pan with foil, with ends of foil extending over sides of pan. Mix cookie crumbs and butter; press firmly onto bottom of prepared pan. Bake 10 minutes.

BEAT cream cheese, sugar and vanilla in large bowl with electric mixer on medium speed until well blended. Add sour cream and chocolate; mix well. Add eggs, 1 at a time, mixing on low speed after each addition just until blended. Pour over crust.

BAKE 40 minutes or until center is almost set. Cool. Refrigerate at least 4 hours or overnight. Lift cheesecake from pan, using foil handles. Top with whipped topping and pie filling. Store any leftover cheesecake in refrigerator.

Makes 16 servings, 1 piece each.

SIZE-WISE:

Sweets can add enjoyment to a balanced diet, but remember to keep tabs on portions.

OREO Cheesecake

Prep: 20 minutes plus refrigerating • Bake: 45 minutes

 1 package (1 pound 2 ounces) **OREO** Chocolate Sandwich Cookies, divided

 ¼ cup (½ stick) butter or margarine, melted

 4 packages (8 ounces each) **PHILADELPHIA** Cream Cheese, softened

 1 cup sugar

 1 teaspoon vanilla

 1 cup **BREAKSTONE'S** or **KNUDSEN** Sour Cream

 4 eggs

PREHEAT oven to 325°F. Line 13×9-inch baking pan with foil, with ends of foil extending over sides of pan. Place 30 cookies in food processor; cover. Process 30 to 45 seconds or until finely ground. Add butter; mix well. Press firmly onto bottom of prepared pan.

BEAT cream cheese, sugar and vanilla in large bowl with electric mixer on medium speed until well blended. Add sour cream; mix well. Add eggs, 1 at a time, beating just until blended after each addition. Chop remaining cookies. Gently stir 1½ cups of the chopped cookies into cream cheese batter. Pour over crust; sprinkle with the remaining chopped cookies.

BAKE 45 minutes or until center is almost set. Cool. Refrigerate 4 hours or overnight. Lift cheesecake from pan, using foil handles. Cut into 16 pieces to serve. Store leftover cheesecake in refrigerator.

Makes 16 servings, 1 piece each.

HOW TO BAKE IN SPRINGFORM PAN:

Preheat oven to 325°F if using a silver 9-inch springform pan (or to 300°F if using a dark nonstick 9-inch springform pan). Prepare crust as directed; press firmly onto bottom of pan. Prepare filling as directed; pour over crust. Sprinkle with chopped cookies as directed. Bake 1 hour or until center is almost set. Run small knife or small spatula around rim of pan to loosen cake; cool before removing rim of pan. Refrigerate 4 hours or overnight.

Chocolate Truffle Cheesecake

Prep: 20 minutes plus refrigerating • Bake: 1 hour 10 minutes

18 **OREO** Chocolate Sandwich Cookies, finely crushed (about 1½ cups crumbs)

2 tablespoons butter or margarine, melted

3 packages (8 ounces each) **PHILADELPHIA** Cream Cheese, softened

1 can (14 ounces) sweetened condensed milk

2 teaspoons vanilla

1 package (12 ounces) **BAKER'S** Semi-Sweet Chocolate Chunks, melted, slightly cooled

4 eggs

PREHEAT oven to 300°F if using silver 9-inch springform pan (or to 275°F if using dark nonstick 9-inch springform pan). Mix cookie crumbs and butter; press firmly onto bottom of pan. Set aside.

BEAT cream cheese, sweetened condensed milk and vanilla in large bowl with electric mixer on medium speed until well blended. Add chocolate; mix well. Add eggs, 1 at a time, mixing on low speed after each addition just until blended. Pour over crust.

BAKE 1 hour 5 minutes to 1 hour 10 minutes or until center is almost set. Run knife or metal spatula around rim of pan to loosen cake; cool before removing rim of pan. Refrigerate at least 4 hours or overnight. Store leftover cheesecake in refrigerator.

Makes 16 servings, 1 slice each.

JAZZ IT UP:

Garnish with fresh raspberries just before serving.

MAKE IT EASY:

Use bottom of straight-sided glass to evenly press cookie crumb mixture onto bottom of springform pan.

JAZZ IT UP:

Add ¼ cup coffee-flavored liqueur along with the chocolate.

best-loved cheesecakes

New York Cappuccino Cheesecake

Prep: 25 minutes plus refrigerating • Bake: 1 hour 10 minutes

- 1 cup chocolate wafer cookie crumbs
- 3 tablespoons sugar
- 2 tablespoons butter or margarine, melted
- 5 packages (8 ounces each) **PHILADELPHIA** Cream Cheese, softened
- 1 cup sugar
- 3 tablespoons flour
- 1 tablespoon vanilla
- 3 eggs
- 1 cup **BREAKSTONE'S** or **KNUDSEN** Sour Cream
- 1 tablespoon **MAXWELL HOUSE** Instant Coffee
- 3 tablespoons coffee-flavored liqueur

PREHEAT oven to 350°F if using a silver 9-inch springform pan (or to 325°F if using a dark nonstick 9-inch springform pan). Mix crumbs, 3 tablespoons sugar and butter; press firmly onto bottom of pan. Bake 10 minutes.

BEAT cream cheese, 1 cup sugar, flour and vanilla in large bowl with electric mixer on medium speed until well blended. Add eggs, 1 at a time, mixing on low speed after each addition just until blended. Add sour cream; mix well. Stir instant coffee granules into liqueur until dissolved. Blend into batter. Pour over crust.

BAKE 1 hour and 5 minutes to 1 hour and 10 minutes or until center is almost set. Run knife or metal spatula around rim of pan to loosen cake; cool before removing rim of pan. Refrigerate 4 hours or overnight. Store leftover cheesecake in refrigerator.

Makes 16 servings.

best-loved cheesecakes

Pumpkin Swirl Cheesecake

Prep: 20 minutes plus refrigerating • Bake: 55 minutes

25 **NABISCO** Ginger Snaps, finely crushed (about 1½ cups)

½ cup finely chopped **PLANTERS** Pecans

¼ cup (½ stick) butter, melted

4 packages (8 ounces each) **PHILADELPHIA** Cream Cheese, softened

1 cup sugar, divided

1 teaspoon vanilla

4 eggs

1 cup canned pumpkin

1 teaspoon ground cinnamon

¼ teaspoon ground nutmeg

Dash ground cloves

PREHEAT oven to 325°F if using a silver 9-inch springform pan (or to 300°F if using a dark nonstick 9-inch springform pan). Mix ginger snap crumbs, pecans and butter; press firmly onto bottom and 1 inch up side of 9-inch springform pan.

BEAT cream cheese, ¾ cup of the sugar and vanilla with electric mixer until well blended. Add eggs, 1 at a time, mixing on low speed after each addition just until blended. Remove 1½ cups batter; place in small bowl. Stir remaining ¼ cup sugar, pumpkin and spices into remaining batter. Spoon half of the pumpkin batter into crust; top with spoonfuls of half of the reserved plain batter. Repeat layers. Cut through batters with knife several times for marble effect.

BAKE 55 minutes or until center is almost set. Cool completely. Refrigerate 4 hours or overnight. Cut into 16 slices. Store leftover cheesecake in refrigerator.

Makes 16 servings, 1 slice each.

HOW TO PREPARE CHEESECAKE IN 13×9-INCH PAN:

Line 13×9-inch baking pan with foil, with ends of foil extending over sides of pan. Prepare cheesecake as directed. Bake at 325°F for 45 minutes.

HOW TO TEST CHEESECAKE DONENESS:

Check cheesecake doneness by gently shaking the pan. If the cheesecake is done, it will be set except for a small area in the center that will be soft and jiggly. Do not insert a knife into the center as this may cause the cheesecake to crack during cooling.

Chocolate Royale Cheesecake Squares

Prep: 20 minutes plus refrigerating • Bake: 50 minutes

- **24** **OREO** Chocolate Sandwich Cookies, crushed (about 2 cups)
- **¼** cup (½ stick) butter or margarine, melted
- **4** packages (8 ounces each) **PHILADELPHIA** Cream Cheese, softened
- **1** cup sugar
- **2** tablespoons flour
- **1** teaspoon vanilla
- **1** package (8 squares) **BAKER'S** Semi-Sweet Baking Chocolate, melted, slightly cooled
- **4** eggs

PREHEAT oven to 325°F. Mix crumbs and butter; press firmly onto bottom of 13×9-inch baking pan. Bake 10 minutes.

BEAT cream cheese, sugar, flour and vanilla in large bowl with electric mixer on medium speed until well blended. Add melted chocolate; mix well. Add eggs, 1 at a time, mixing on low speed after each addition just until blended. Pour over crust.

BAKE 45 to 50 minutes or until center is almost set. Refrigerate at least 4 hours or overnight. Cut into 32 squares to serve. Store leftover dessert squares in refrigerator.

Makes 32 servings, 1 square each.

HOW TO PRESS CRUMB MIXTURE INTO PAN TO MAKE CRUST:

Use bottom of a dry measuring cup to evenly press cookie crumb mixture onto bottom of pan.

JAZZ IT UP:

Garnish with sifted powdered sugar and mixed berries just before serving, if desired.

JAZZ IT UP:

Add ¼ cup hazelnut liqueur with the melted chocolate.

best-loved cheesecakes

New York-Style
Sour Cream-Topped Cheesecake

Prep: 15 minutes plus refrigerating • Bake: 40 minutes

1½ cups **HONEY MAID** Graham Cracker Crumbs

¼ cup (½ stick) butter, melted

1¼ cups sugar, divided

4 packages (8 ounces each) **PHILADELPHIA** Cream Cheese, softened

2 teaspoons vanilla, divided

1 container (16 ounces) **BREAKSTONE'S** or **KNUDSEN** Sour Cream, divided

4 eggs

PREHEAT oven to 325°F. Line 13×9-inch baking pan with foil, with ends of foil extending over sides of pan. Mix crumbs, butter and 2 tablespoons of the sugar; press firmly onto bottom of prepared pan.

BEAT cream cheese, 1 cup of the remaining sugar and 1 teaspoon of the vanilla in large bowl with electric mixer on medium speed until well blended. Add 1 cup of the sour cream; mix well. Add eggs, one at a time, beating on low speed after each addition just until blended. Pour over crust.

BAKE 40 minutes or until center is almost set. Mix remaining sour cream, 2 tablespoons sugar and 1 teaspoon vanilla until well blended; carefully spread over cheesecake. Bake an additional 10 minutes. Cool. Cover; refrigerate 4 hours or overnight. Lift cheesecake from pan, using foil handles. Garnish as desired. Store leftover cheesecake in refrigerator.

Makes 16 servings, 1 piece each.

SUBSTITUTE:

Prepare as directed, substituting 1½ cups finely crushed OREO Chocolate Sandwich Cookies for the graham cracker crumbs.

HEALTHY LIVING:

Great news! You'll save 80 calories, 9 grams of fat and 7 grams of saturated fat per serving by preparing with margarine, PHILADELPHIA Neufchâtel Cheese, ⅓ Less Fat than Cream Cheese and BREAKSTONE'S Reduced Fat or KNUDSEN Light Sour Cream (for a delicious 340 calories and 21 grams of fat per serving).

PARTY LINE

APPETIZERS, DIPS, AND SMALL BITES
PERFECT FOR ENTERTAINING

BLT Dip

Prep: 15 minutes

- 1 package (8 ounces) **PHILADELPHIA** Cream Cheese, softened
- ¾ cup shredded or chopped romaine lettuce
- 2 plum tomatoes, seeded, chopped
- 4 slices **OSCAR MAYER** Bacon, crisply cooked, drained and crumbled

SPREAD cream cheese onto bottom of 9-inch pie plate.

TOP with lettuce and tomatoes; sprinkle with bacon.

SERVE with **WHEAT THINS** Snack Crackers or assorted cut-up fresh vegetables.

Makes 2 cups or 16 servings, 2 tablespoons each.

VARIATION:

Prepare as directed, using PHILADELPHIA Neufchâtel Cheese, ⅓ Less Fat than Cream Cheese and LOUIS RICH Turkey Bacon.

Sweet Fruit Dip

Prep: 10 minutes plus refrigerating

4 ounces (½ of 8-ounce package) **PHILADELPHIA** Cream Cheese, softened

1 cup whole berry cranberry sauce

1 cup thawed **COOL WHIP** Whipped Topping

BEAT cream cheese and cranberry sauce with electric mixer on medium speed until well blended. Gently stir in whipped topping; cover.

REFRIGERATE at least 1 hour or until ready to serve.

SERVE with strawberries, red and green grapes, pineapple, kiwi or pears, cut into bite-size pieces for dipping.

Makes 16 servings, 2 tablespoons each.

FUN IDEA:

This dip is great spooned over individual servings of cut-up fresh fruit.

SUBSTITUTE:

Prepare as directed, using PHILADELPHIA Neufchâtel Cheese, ⅓ Less Fat than Cream Cheese and COOL WHIP LITE Whipped Topping.

Cheesy Chili Dip

Prep: 5 minutes • Microwave: 1 minute

- **1** package (8 ounces) **PHILADELPHIA** Cream Cheese, softened
- **1** can (15 ounces) chili
- **½** cup **KRAFT** Shredded Cheddar Cheese
- **2** tablespoons chopped cilantro

SPREAD cream cheese onto bottom of microwaveable pie plate; top with chili and Cheddar cheese.

MICROWAVE on HIGH (100%) 45 seconds to 1 minute or until Cheddar cheese is melted. Sprinkle with cilantro.

SERVE with **RITZ** Crackers.

Makes 3 cups or 24 servings, 2 tablespoons each.

SERVE AS A TOPPER:

Place unwrapped block of cream cheese on microwaveable plate; top with chili and Cheddar cheese. Microwave and garnish with cilantro before serving as directed.

VARIATION:

Use your favorite variety of canned chili, with or without beans, regular or spicy.

Mexican Dip

Prep: 10 minutes

1 package (8 ounces) **PHILADELPHIA** Neufchâtel Cheese, ⅓ Less Fat than
    Cream Cheese, softened

½ cup **TACO BELL HOME ORIGINALS** Salsa

½ cup **KRAFT** 2% Milk Shredded Reduced Fat Cheddar Cheese

2 green onions, sliced (about ¼ cup)

   WHEAT THINS Reduced Fat Baked Snack Crackers

SPREAD Neufchâtel cheese onto bottom of 9-inch pie plate.

TOP with layers of salsa, Cheddar cheese and onions.

SERVE with the crackers.

Makes 1⅔ cups dip or 13 servings, 2 tablespoons dip and 16 crackers each.

HOW TO SOFTEN NEUFCHÂTEL CHEESE:

Place unwrapped package of Neufchâtel cheese on microwaveable plate. Microwave on
HIGH (100%) 20 to 30 seconds or until slightly softened.

TACO BELL Logo and HOME ORIGINALS are trademarks owned and licensed by Taco Bell Corp.

Tomato-Basil Dip

Prep: 10 minutes

- **1** package (8 ounces) **PHILADELPHIA** Neufchâtel Cheese, ⅓ Less Fat than Cream Cheese, softened
- **2** plum tomatoes, seeded, chopped
- **2** tablespoons **KRAFT** Zesty Italian Dressing
- **2** tablespoons **KRAFT** Shredded Parmesan Cheese
- **1** tablespoons finely chopped fresh basil

SPREAD Neufchâtel cheese onto bottom of 9-inch pie plate.

MIX tomatoes and dressing; spoon over Neufchâtel cheese. Sprinkle with the Parmesan cheese and basil.

SERVE with **WHEAT THINS** Snack Crackers or assorted cut-up fresh vegetables.

Makes 1¾ cups or 14 servings, 2 tablespoons each.

VARIATION:

Prepare as directed, substituting KRAFT Balsamic Vinaigrette Dressing for Italian dressing.

Shrimp Cocktail Dip

Prep: 10 minutes

- **1** package (8 ounces) **PHILADELPHIA** Cream Cheese, softened
- **¾** pound cooked shrimp, chopped (about 2 cups)
- **¾** cup **KRAFT** Cocktail Sauce
- **¼** cup **KRAFT** Shredded Parmesan Cheese
- **¼** cup sliced green onions

SPREAD cream cheese onto bottom of 9-inch pie plate. Toss shrimp with cocktail sauce; spoon over cream cheese.

SPRINKLE with Parmesan cheese and onions.

SERVE with **WHEAT THINS** Snack Crackers.

Makes 3 cups or 24 servings, 2 tablespoons each.

SUBSTITUTE:

Substitute 1 package (8 ounces) imitation crabmeat, coarsely chopped, for shrimp.

Creamy Coconut Dip

1 package (8 ounces) **PHILADELPHIA** Cream Cheese, softened

1 can (15 ounces) cream of coconut

1 tub (16 ounces) **COOL WHIP** Whipped Topping, thawed

BEAT cream cheese and cream of coconut in large bowl with wire whisk until well blended.

ADD whipped topping; gently stir until well blended. Cover. Refrigerate several hours or until chilled.

SERVE with **HONEY MAID** Grahams Honey Sticks, **HONEY MAID** Honey Grahams or cut-up fresh fruit.

Makes 48 servings, 2 tablespoons each.

JAZZ IT UP:

Garnish with toasted BAKER'S ANGEL FLAKE Coconut just before serving.

Garden Vegetable Dip

Prep: 10 minutes plus refrigerating

- 2 packages (8 ounces each) **PHILADELPHIA** Cream Cheese, softened
- ½ cup **KRAFT** Blue Cheese Dressing
- ½ cup finely chopped broccoli
- 1 medium carrot, shredded

MIX cream cheese and dressing until well blended. Stir in vegetables; cover.

REFRIGERATE several hours or until chilled.

SERVE with assorted **NABISCO** Crackers.

Makes 20 servings, 2 tablespoons each.

BEST OF SEASON:

Take advantage of the fresh seasonal vegetables that are available. Cut up zucchini, cucumbers and bell peppers to serve as dippers with this creamy dip.

VARIATION:

Prepare as directed, using **PHILADELPHIA** Neufchâtel Cheese, ⅓ Less Fat than Cream Cheese and **KRAFT** Light Blue Cheese Reduced Fat Dressing.

Bacon Appetizer Crescents

Prep: 30 minutes • Bake: 15 minutes

 1 package (8 ounces) **PHILADELPHIA** Cream Cheese, softened

 8 slices **OSCAR MAYER** Bacon, crisply cooked, crumbled

 ⅓ cup **KRAFT** 100% Grated Parmesan Cheese

 ¼ cup finely chopped onion

 2 tablespoons chopped fresh parsley

 1 tablespoon milk

 2 cans (8 ounces each) refrigerated crescent dinner rolls

PREHEAT oven to 375°F. Mix cream cheese, bacon, Parmesan cheese, onions, parsley and milk until well blended; set aside.

SEPARATE each can of dough into 8 triangles. Spread each triangle with 1 rounded tablespoonful of cream cheese mixture. Cut each triangle lengthwise into 3 narrow triangles. Roll up, starting at wide ends. Place point-side down on greased baking sheet.

BAKE 12 to 15 minutes or until golden brown. Serve warm.

Makes 4 dozen or 24 servings, 2 crescents each.

JAZZ IT UP:

Sprinkle lightly with poppy seeds before baking.

Mini New Potato Bites

Prep: 30 minutes plus refrigerating

1½ **pounds new potatoes (about 15 potatoes)**

4 **ounces (½ of 8-ounce package) PHILADELPHIA Cream Cheese, softened**

2 **tablespoons BREAKSTONE'S or KNUDSEN Sour Cream**

2 **tablespoons KRAFT 100% Grated Parmesan Cheese**

4 **slices OSCAR MAYER Bacon, cooked, crumbled**

2 **tablespoons snipped fresh chives**

PLACE potatoes in large saucepan; add enough water to cover. Bring to boil. Reduce heat to medium-low; cook 15 minutes or until potatoes are tender.

MEANWHILE, mix cream cheese, sour cream and Parmesan cheese; cover. Refrigerate until ready to use.

DRAIN potatoes. Cool slightly. Cut potatoes in half; cut small piece from bottom of each potato half so potato lies flat. Place on serving platter. Top each potato half with 1 teaspoon of the cream cheese mixture. Sprinkle with bacon and chives.

Makes 15 servings, 2 topped potato halves each.

MAKE AHEAD:

These potatoes are delicious served hot or cold.

SUBSTITUTE:

Substitute PHILADELPHIA Chive & Onion Cream Cheese Spread for the regular cream cheese for added flavor.

Three Pepper Quesadillas

Prep: 20 minutes • Bake: 10 minutes

- 1 cup thin green bell pepper strips
- 1 cup thin red bell pepper strips
- 1 cup thin yellow bell pepper strips
- ½ cup thin onion slices
- ⅓ cup butter or margarine
- ½ teaspoon ground cumin
- 1 package (8 ounces) **PHILADELPHIA** Cream Cheese, softened
- 1 package (8 ounces) **KRAFT** Shredded Sharp Cheddar Cheese
- 10 **TACO BELL HOME ORIGINALS** Flour Tortillas
- 1 jar (16 ounces) **TACO BELL HOME ORIGINALS** Thick 'N Chunky Salsa

PREHEAT oven to 425°F. Cook and stir peppers and onion in butter in large skillet on medium-high heat until crisp-tender. Stir in cumin. Drain, reserving liquid.

BEAT cream cheese and Cheddar cheese with electric mixer on medium speed until well blended. Spoon 2 tablespoons cheese mixture onto each tortilla; top each evenly with pepper mixture. Fold tortillas in half; place on ungreased baking sheet. Brush with reserved liquid.

BAKE 10 minutes or until heated through. Cut each tortilla into thirds. Serve warm with salsa.

Makes 30 servings, 1 piece each.

MAKE AHEAD:

Prepare as directed except for baking; cover. Refrigerate. When ready to serve, bake, uncovered, at 425°F for 15 to 20 minutes or until heated through.

Blue Cheese Mushrooms

Prep: 30 minutes • Broil: 3 minutes

 1 **pound medium fresh mushrooms**

 ¼ **cup sliced green onions**

 1 **tablespoon butter or margarine**

 1 **package (4 ounces) ATHENOS Crumbled Blue Cheese**

 3 **ounces PHILADELPHIA Cream Cheese, softened**

PREHEAT broiler. Remove stems from mushrooms; chop stems. Cook and stir stems and onions in butter in small skillet on medium heat until tender.

ADD blue cheese and cream cheese; mix well. Spoon evenly into mushroom caps; place on rack of broiler pan.

BROIL 2 to 3 minutes or until golden brown. Serve warm.

Makes about 2 dozen or 24 servings, 1 mushroom each.

Baked Crab Rangoon

Prep: 20 minutes • Bake: 20 minutes

- **1** can (6 ounces) white crabmeat, drained, flaked
- **4** ounces (½ of 8-ounce package) **PHILADELPHIA** Neufchâtel Cheese, ⅓ Less Fat than Cream Cheese, softened
- **¼** cup thinly sliced green onions
- **¼** cup **KRAFT** Mayo Light Mayonnaise
- **12** wonton wrappers

PREHEAT oven to 350°F. Mix crabmeat, Neufchâtel cheese, onions and mayo.

SPRAY 12 medium muffin cups with cooking spray. Gently place 1 wonton wrapper in each cup, allowing edges of wrappers to extend above sides of cups. Fill evenly with crabmeat mixture.

BAKE 18 to 20 minutes or until edges are golden brown and filling is heated through. Serve warm. Garnish with sliced green onions, if desired.

Makes 12 servings, 1 wonton each.

FOOD FACTS:

Wonton wrappers are usually found in the grocery store in the refrigerated section of the produce department.

FOR MINI CRAB RANGOONS:

Use 24 wonton wrappers. Gently place 1 wonton wrapper in each of 24 miniature muffin cups sprayed with cooking spray. Fill evenly with crabmeat mixture and bake as directed. Makes 12 servings, 2 appetizers each.

Party Cheese Ball

Prep: 15 minutes plus refrigerating

2 packages (8 ounces each) **PHILADELPHIA** Cream Cheese, softened

1 package (8 ounces) **KRAFT** Shredded Sharp Cheddar Cheese

1 tablespoon finely chopped onions

1 tablespoon chopped red bell peppers

2 teaspoons Worcestershire sauce

1 teaspoon lemon juice

   Dash ground red pepper (cayenne)

   Dash salt

1 cup chopped **PLANTERS** Pecans

BEAT cream cheese and Cheddar cheese in small bowl with electric mixer on medium speed until well blended.

MIX in all remaining ingredients except pecans; cover. Refrigerate several hours or overnight.

SHAPE into ball; roll in pecans. Serve with assorted **NABISCO** Crackers.

Makes 24 servings, 2 tablespoons each.

VARIATION:

Mix cream cheese mixture as directed; shape into log or 24 small balls, each about 1 inch in diameter. Roll in pecans until evenly coated. Serve as directed.

SUBSTITUTE:

Substitute pimientos for the red bell peppers.

Deviled Ham Finger Sandwiches

Prep: 15 minutes

- 1 package (8 ounces) **PHILADELPHIA** Cream Cheese, softened
- 1 can (4.25 ounces) deviled ham
- ¼ cup **KRAFT** Mayo Real Mayonnaise
- 10 small stuffed green olives, finely chopped
- 36 slices white bread, crusts removed

MIX cream cheese, ham, mayo and olives until well blended.

SPREAD each of 18 of the bread slices with about 2 tablespoons of the cream cheese mixture. Cover with remaining bread slices to make 18 sandwiches.

CUT each sandwich into quarters.

Makes 18 servings, 4 sandwich quarters each.

MAKE AHEAD:

Prepare cream cheese mixture as directed. Cover and refrigerate up to 5 days. Spread onto bread slices and continue as directed. For easier spreading, mix 1 tablespoon milk with chilled cream cheese mixture before spreading onto bread slices. Or prepare sandwiches as directed, but do not cut into quarters. Wrap in plastic wrap. Refrigerate until ready to serve. Cut into quarters just before serving.

SUBSTITUTE:

Substitute MIRACLE WHIP Dressing for the mayo.

Savory Bruschetta

Prep: 25 minutes

¼ cup olive oil

1 clove garlic, minced

1 loaf (1 pound) French bread, cut in half lengthwise

1 package (8 ounces) **PHILADELPHIA** Cream Cheese, softened

3 tablespoons **KRAFT** 100% Grated Parmesan Cheese

2 tablespoons chopped pitted ripe olives

1 cup chopped, seeded plum tomatoes

¼ cup chopped fresh basil

PREHEAT oven to 400°F. Mix oil and garlic; spread onto cut surfaces of bread. Bake 8 to 10 minutes or until lightly browned. Cool.

MIX cream cheese and Parmesan cheese with electric mixer on medium speed until blended. Stir in olives.

SPREAD toasted bread halves with cream cheese mixture; top with tomatoes. Cut into 24 slices to serve. Sprinkle with basil.

Makes 2 dozen or 24 servings, 1 slice each.

SHORTCUT:

Prepare as directed, using 1 can (14½ ounces) diced tomatoes, drained, for the chopped fresh tomatoes.